Our Neighborhood at Work

A Division of The McGraw-Hill Companies

Columbus, Ohio

— PROGRAM AUTHORS —

Marilyn Jager Adams · Anne McKeough · Marlene Scardamalia
Carl Bereiter · Michael Pressley · Gerald H. Treadway, Jr.
Jan Hirshberg · Marsha Roit · Marcy Stein

Acknowledgments

Grateful acknowledgment is given to the following publishers and copyright owners for permissions granted to reprint selections from their publications. All possible care has been taken to trace ownership and secure permission for each selection included. In case of any errors or omissions, the Publisher will be pleased to make suitable acknowledgments in future editions.

GUESS WHO? COPYRIGHT © 1994 BY MARGARET MILLER. Used by permission of HarperCollins Publishers.

FIREFIGHTERS by Jan Mader. Used by permission of the author.

WORKSONG, text copyright © 1997 by Gary Paulsen, illustrations copyright © 1997 by Ruth Wright Paulsen, reprinted with permission of Harcourt Inc.

Photo Credits

4-23 © Margaret Miller; 24-47 © Justin Shady; 64 (tl) Gift of Edsel B. Ford, The Detroit Institute of Arts, Detroit, Michigan. Photograph © 1996, (r) Christie's Images, (bl) Art Resource, NY.

www.sra4kids.com

SRA/McGraw-Hill

A Division of The McGraw·Hill Companies

Send all inquiries to:
SRA/McGraw-Hill
8787 Orion Place
Columbus, Ohio 43240-4027

Printed in Mexico

ISBN 0-07-602724-4

5 6 7 8 9 DRN 10

Table of Contents
Our Neighborhood at Work

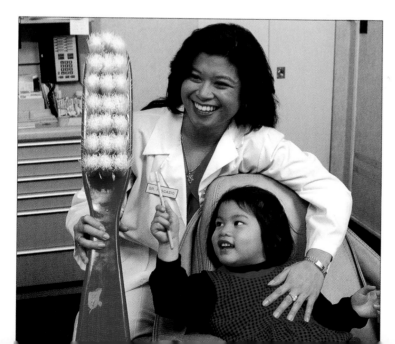

Focus Questions What job do you want to have when you get older? What kinds of work do people do in your neighborhood?

Guess Who?

Margaret Miller

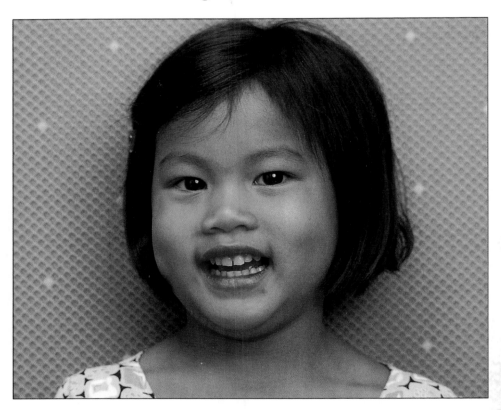

Who cleans your teeth?

A cat?

A shoemaker?

A window washer?

A rubber duckie?

A dentist!

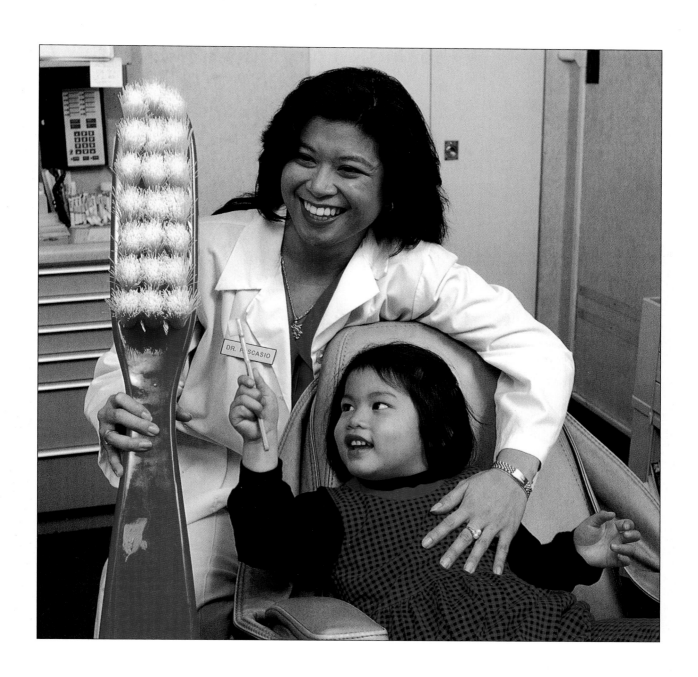

Who flies an airplane?

A bus driver?

A statue?

A turtle?

A baby?

A pilot!

Who makes your bread?

A giraffe?

A juggler?

An artist?

A potter?

13

A baker!

Who fixes your car?

A crab?

A plumber?

A clown?

A veterinarian?

A mechanic!

Who delivers your mail?

A magician?

A pitcher?

A police officer?

A parrot?

21

A letter carrier!

Firefighters

Jan Mader
photography by Justin Shady

This book is dedicated to hardworking firefighters everywhere. Special thanks to Lt. John Hill.

Inside Station 1 at 8:00 each morning roll call is taken. The firefighters live at the fire station for 24 hours at a time and there are many things to do.

One of the firefighters is the cook. He collects money from each person and goes to the grocery store to buy enough food for the whole crew.

Some firefighters think that the cook
has the most important job at the station.

Other firefighters work together to keep the fire station sparkling clean. The fire trucks are washed every morning, and the other equipment is cleaned and checked regularly, too.

A watchman answers the phone.
He keeps track of each emergency run,
monitors the radio, and greets visitors.

Firefighters study and learn new things all the time. Some days are spent in classes at the station, learning about hazardous materials, electricity, maps and many other things.

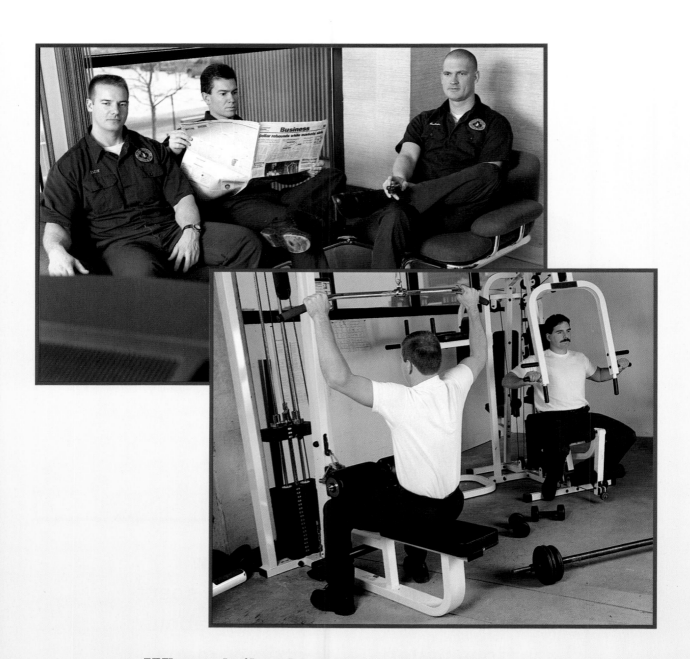

When daily chores are done the
firefighters can exercise or watch TV.

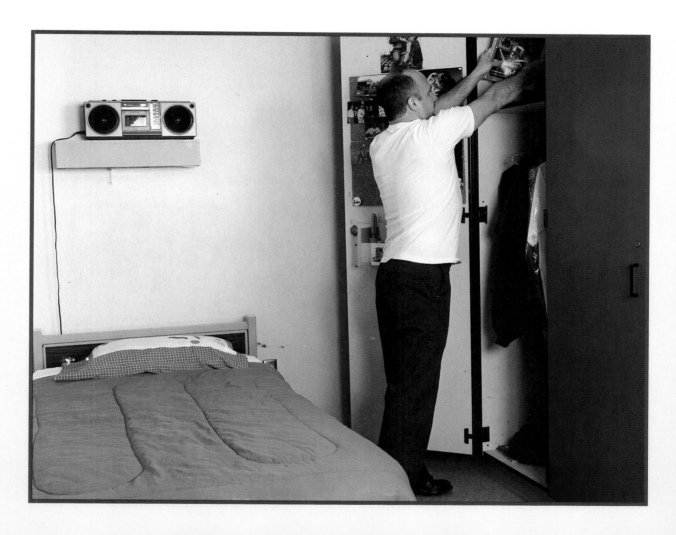

At night, after ten o'clock, the firefighters can take catnaps in their dorm rooms.

But when the fire alarm sounds, the firefighters must drop everything and rush to their trucks.

Many fire stations have poles to help the firefighters get to the bay where the fire trucks are waiting. It is much faster to slide down a pole than to run down steps.

Firefighters know the best way to control a fire is to get to the fire fast. The firefighters' gear is kept right by the fire trucks so they can get dressed quickly.

All firefighters wear heavy coats, hats, boots and gloves to protect them from water, fire and falling objects.

Each firefighter has a special place on one of the huge fire trucks. Some of the fire trucks are so big, two firefighters drive.

One driver is in the front of the truck
and one driver is at the back.

As soon as they reach the fire, the firefighters go to work. The firefighters know just what to do.

They use walkie-talkies to keep in touch with one another. The chief can use his walkie-talkie to call for more firefighters and trucks if he needs extra help.

Firefighters carry tanks of air on their backs so they can breathe when the smoke is very thick.

The most important job is to save lives.
A platform ladder can carry a firefighter
7 or 8 stories high.

The members of the ladder company break holes in the roof or smash the windows of a burning house to release the fire and smoke trapped inside. This makes it easier to fight the fire and rescue people.

Some firefighters attach lines to pumper trucks. The pumper truck pumps the water from the closest fire hydrant into the hoses (called lines).

Then the firefighters aim streams of water at the flames.

After the fire is out, it is time to clean up. Firefighters search for live embers or sparks. They might have to tear down walls and ceilings, just to make sure the fire doesn't start again.

The firefighters return to Station 1.
They are ready for the next fire.

The firefighters are proud of their work.

Worksong

Gary Paulsen

illustrated by Ruth Wright Paulsen

It is keening noise and jolting sights,

and hammers flashing in the light,

and houses up and trees in sun,

and trucks on one more nighttime run.

It is fresh new food to fill the plates,

and flat, clean sidewalks to try to skate,
and towering buildings that were not there,
hanging suddenly in the air.

It is offices filled with glowing screens

and workers making steel beams,

and ice-cream cones to lick and wear,

and all the pins that hold
your hair.

It's gentle arms that lift and hold,

and all the soldiers brave and bold,

and help to fit the
brand-new shoes,

and hands to show you books to use.

It is people here and people there,
making things for all to share;

all the things there are to be,
and nearly all there is to see.

And when the day is paid and done,

and all the errands have been run,

it's mother, father in a chair,
with tired eyes and loosened hair.

Resting short but
loving long,

resting for the next day's song.

Our Neighborhood at Work

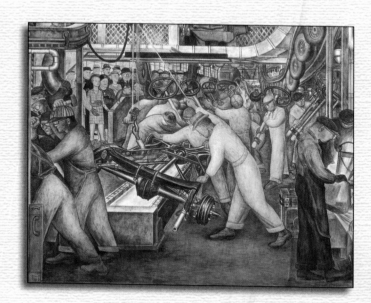

Detail of Detroit Industry, South Wall. 1932–33. **Diego M. Rivera.** Fresco. The Detroit Institute of Arts, Detroit, Michigan.

In the Barbershop. 1934. **Ilya Bolotowsky.** National Museum of American Art, Smithsonian Institution, Washington, DC. ©Estate of Ilya Bolotowsky/Licensed by VAGA, New York.

Moving Day. 1968. **William Roberts.** Private Collection.

Glossary

A

An **artist** is painting a picture in the park.

C

Carlos took a **catnap** before going to soccer practice.

D

We go to a **dentist** to have our teeth checked two times each year.

E

Even though the fire was out, there were still **embers** in the fireplace.

F

The candle **flame** gave off some light when the power went out.

G

Lightning bugs **glow** at night.

H

To get the nails out of the wall, Mom will use a **hammer.**

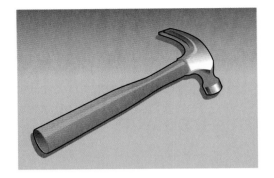

Hazardous materials must be handled very carefully.

M

The **mechanic** is fixing the car this week.

P

When I grow up, I want to be a **pilot** so I can fly planes.

The firefighters will use a **platform ladder** to help the people in the apartments.

Firefighters use a **pole** to get to their fire trucks quickly.

The **police officer** rides her bike around town in the afternoon.

Firefighters use a **pumper truck** to pump water from a fire hydrant.

S

The bigger computer **screen** is easier to read.

Mom took her shoes to a **shoemaker** to be fixed.

There was a lot of **smoke** coming from the campfire.

T

The truck is **towering** over the car on the highway.

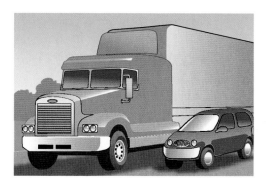

V

Our new kitty saw the **veterinarian.**

W

When Michael comes over to play, we like to use our **walkie-talkies.**

A **watchman** guards the building at night.